HAVING WITNESSED THE ILLUSION

POEMS
NICOLE GREAVES

GLASS LYRE PRESS

Copyright © 2022 Nicole Greaves
Paperback ISBN: 978-1-941783-86-3

All rights reserved: Except for the purpose of quoting brief passages for review, no part of this book may be reproduced or transmitted in any form or by any means, electronic or mechanical, including photocopying, recording, or by any information storage and retrieval system, without permission in writing from the publisher.

Design & Layout: Steven Asmussen
Cover Art: Iris Hills
Author Photo: Eva O'Melvin

Glass Lyre Press, LLC
P.O. Box 2693
Glenview, IL 60025
www.GlassLyrePress.com

Having Witnessed the Illusion

Gratitudes

Because a book is a group project

Immense gratitude to the Glass Lyre Editors and staff for their guidance and care of my work. Glass Lyre's mission speaks to the heart of who I am as a poet and a person, and I could not be more honored to be represented by this press.

I am eternally grateful to Virginia Konchan's and Amy Small-McKinney's guidance over the past few years as I have stitched this book together. To Virginia for her inquiry-based feedback, which deepened my relationship with individual poems as I whittled them to precision. To dear Amy for permitting me to claim myself and my voice in this book, and for her endless scholarship, wit, and love.

To E. Beth Thomas for her keen eye, which helped me polish this work, and for her continued encouragement and counsel for the last twenty-five-plus years.

To my writers' group, Scribes: Carol Coffin, Paige Menton, & Barbara Hoekje. Our monthly meetings have sustained me as a poet, mother, thinker, and teacher.

To all my poetry teachers, especially Lucie Brock-Broido, Bill Knott, J. D. McClatchy, Molly Peacock, and Peter Shippy. I work each day to share your wisdom forward and honor the time you took to nurture my voice and soul.

To my girlhood best friend, Emily Bumble Frogget, who shared my dream to write and with whom the narratives began to take shape.

To all my other friends in poetry, especially Liz Ahl, Scott Hightower, Major Jackson, Elline Lipkin, Joanne Leva, Christopher Patton, Michelle Reale, Nora Wright, and Mark Wunderlich.

To all the editors who gave my poems a home and nominated my work for prizes.

To my former student Iris Hills for designing my gorgeous website and creating the book's cover art. You never cease to amaze me.

To The Crefeld School and my esteemed colleagues, past and present, who always support and celebrate my work.

To my students, who inspire me every day to be a better writer, poet, and teacher.

To my children, Liam and Eva, who inspire so many of my musings. Eva, your humor and zeal helped me persist and laugh at myself. Liam, your intellect, sense of language, and understanding of art opened my mind to new possibilities in the text. To my husband, Chris, for enduring the chaos that is putting together a book and for believing in me.

To my extended family and friends, I cannot thank you enough for your enthusiasm and love.

To my ancestors, I am forever indebted to you, especially the women.

Mostly, to my late mother, known as Nina, born Josefa Virzi de Herrera in Santiago, Panama, in 1943 and who emigrated to the US in 1960. She raised me on her own, and so much of this book speaks to our deep connection. Thank you for being my first scribe. *Te amo, Mamá.*

Acknowledgments

Much gratitude to the editors of the following journals and magazines, where versions of these poems appeared.

The Acentos Review: "Conventicle," "Mine," "Head to the Wind," and "By the Trolley Line"

American Poetry Review, Philly Edition: "My Mother Brings Her Social Work Home Because When It Happens It Happens Every Day"

The Avatar Review: "When We Were Immortal," "After the Miscarriage, I Drove to the Playground," "Prelude," and "When You Find My Neighbor Elena, She'll Be Wearing the Classic Black Dress"

Cleaver Magazine: "Moments in the Trees" and "Sack of Scarabs"

Friends Journal: "Faith and Practice"

Radar Poetry: "Awakening to My Mother's Voice from Beyond," "Child on a Tricycle," "Having Witnessed the Illusion," "My Mother's Dresden Teacup" (nominated for Best of the Net), "The Rhyme Game," and "Because We Are Planets Swarming with Life," finalists for the Coniston Prize

Rag Queen Periodical: "Heidi's Hair Like Ivy" and "Learning Silence"

Matter: "At Fifteen," "You Will Learn Some Lessons Along the Way," and "Over the Waves"

Schuylkill Valley Journal: "The Quarry Inside Me"

CONTENTS

Gratitudes   v
Acknowledgments   vii

I. Another Country

Prelude   1
Conventicle   2
Sack of Scarabs   3
Mine   4
Head to the Wind   5
My Mother Brings Her Social Work Home
    Because When It Happens It Happens Every Day   6
You Will Learn Some Lessons Along the Way   8
With My Sacred Heart   9
At Fifteen   11
The Tethering Post   12
Caning   13
Latchkey 1   15
When You Find My Neighbor Elena,
    She'll Be Wearing the Classic Black Dress   16
Heidi's Hair Like Ivy   18
Safe in the Kitchen   19
The Compact   20
Writing Her Dissertation   21
My Mother's Dresden Teacup   22
By the Trolley Line   24
Souvenir   25

II. The Waiting Room

Having Witnessed the Illusion	29
Through the Lens	30
The Hour	31
My Mother and I Tour the World While She Is Dying	32
The Scrimshaw Begins to Glow in the Sun, on the Bedside Table	33
The Eye Exam	34
Her Life on the Wall	35
Notes from the Forest	36
MRI	37
The Streak	38
Child on a Tricycle	39
Latchkey 2	40
After the Miscarriage, I Drove to the Playground	41
When My Mother Is Weeks Away from Leaving, Her Client Calls Her for Counsel	42
Dying in Winter	44
Moments in the Trees	45
Learning Silence	46
Over the Waves	47
My Mother Will Never Leave the Room Alive Again	48

III. Reclaimed

Ticonderoga	51
My Son Learns Art Can Save Him	52
The Quarry Inside Me	53
Driving By	54
Awakening to My Mother's Voice from Beyond	55
The Flora Print Still Hangs Above Her Bed	56
Mi Casa	57
Votives	58
Final Receipt	59
My Daughter Is Spending the Rest of the Summer in Her Room	60
Reclaimed	61
Because We Are Planets Swarming with Life	62
Faith and Practice	63
Carnival	64
The Rhyme Game	65
Canción	68
The Descendants	69
When We Were Immortal	70
Fridays, I Stop to Read Their Journals	71
Candlemas	72
Sorting Through My Inheritance	73
Epilogue	75
Notes	77
About the Author	81

"Thus they went on living in a reality that was slipping away, momentarily captured by words, but which would escape irremediably when they forgot the values of the written letters."

— Gabriel García Márquez, *One Hundred Years of Solitude*

For my mother, Nina Virzi, 1943-2010

I. Another Country

Prelude

There was a year when you thought of nothing
but horses, from the wild mustang to thoroughbreds, some white

but mostly you envisioned them dark, chestnut and black,
shiny like light on the surface of water. Cutouts

covered your walls, until there was only them
falling into each other: how could there be anything else

to dream of? You wore your hair like a mane,
braided like a mane, like a rope running down

behind you. For a year you felt too massive to stay,
too wounded to move forward. You listened for bells,

for the precision in a sentence that held the shape of an arrow,
one that knew how to find the heart, as if the heart were truly

forgiveness. It was then you began to realize that there might be others
who thought they could become horses too, and you called to them,

and sometimes you believed you heard them answer,
as an afterthought, while trying to leave this world for the next.

Conventicle

—Panama, 1992

Moonlight, the crack of stone
inside a hidden doorway, rooms

of dust, of cotton. Two women
sing behind adobe walls, prayer

for Maria, prayer for the wedded
woman sitting alone in the dark,

full with water. They know this:
slow needlework, twine lined

with cloth, pots burned with rice.
I look through the windows, the light

chisels each round face, each
round body. There are no men

for miles, only us, here
in this country between countries,

in this light of refuge,
in this nightly covenant.

Sack of Scarabs

The museum's glass box was hidden from light
in between the hopeful columns, the scarabs swarming in a pool
of fabric. Somehow they made the presence of my mother's body
more familiar, in the way her shadow made it more foreign.

It takes a distraction to move us
further from ourselves, at the same time, closer;
it's the sickness of the mirror, how it moves
from reflection to the well, to reflection again.

My mother and I held hands as we walked, lest one of us be lost
to the museum—and part of us is still there
—the thin wrap of my wrist against hers
like plagiarism, the rooms cool around us like wet paint.

When she said my name it rose like a balloon
in a circus tent. Those scarabs pressing against glass
like my children's faces to animal stunts, like my own
against my mother's waist, its yeasty scent.

The scarabs' color, the imitation that longs
for its sea. A line dividing them, an aquiline nose.
It was getting late, the day descended like the hood
of a jump rope over my eight-year-old body.

I knew we would be the last ones left in the rooms—
it was the usual case—and if not for the announcer's voice,
a woman's shoes clicking like coughs, like my mother's
surgical heartbeat—we might not have noticed our own need

to leave and gone on for hours, training from one display
to another, stopping again at the sack of scarabs
in their square box, the shape the world was once regarded
to be. Me on tippy-toes, as if on the high dive, beginning to fall.

Mine

Through the keyhole of my ear
where I was locked in
to what my mother and tía
were saying, the disagreement
of their silhouettes
in their first language,
language of sails and conquest,
where *azul* is closer
to the blue in fire,
hija closer
to the thread in daughter,
and *mía* closer to mine,
the first word I would learn
in their language,
what I would say
as I touched things—
though their language
was not what I was given.

Head to the Wind

It was temporary in a sea of temporaries that became the permanence of home, between what had happened and what came next that was the waiting for our proverbial ship to come in, like those tall ships that roamed colonial ports trying to catch up to us, or was it us trying to catch up to them? *We were always missing that hope.* My mother was always mixing up her idioms: *A bucket will drop, so make your bed. You are the eye of my apple. Don't look a dark horse in the mouth.*

My mother's work was social work, and there we were living in it. Their Elvis or Jackson 5 on one side of the wall. Her Simon and Garfunkel, and sometimes salsa and cumbia, on our side. A dueling conversation that no one picked up in the morning.

That September I wore a blue sweater, the exact color of blueberries, with a bit of purple that rose to the edge as it does under skin, after falling. I wore it each day so that someone called me *Blueberry Girl*, and it took. *Blueberry Girl* getting the newspaper and coffee in the motel lobby. *Blueberry Girl* holding her cousin's hand to the bus stop. *Niña Arándano*, with a nod and a wink.

Out of the blue, my cousin's father visited one day and brought her a doll head for styling her hair and painting her face, a face so pale it seemed to radiate at night, catching the streetlamps on the dresser like a figurehead on a ship's prow taking us across the sea. I curled up tightly next to my mother in bed, felt her calloused feet, and longed to sand them down, to whittle at them as if they were wood, to turn them into birds.

My Mother Brings Her Social Work Home Because When It Happens It Happens Every Day

The seam of her coat ripped
in winter. The music box silent
since Abuela died. No pills in the medicine cabinet.
Red wine in the refrigerator.
Her ear against a glass hears the rumba next door
and Junior pounding his feet against wood.

Through the window
she watches the lady down the street
catch cats and pigeons, Junior says for dinner.
On her knees she bends to kiss
Mama's head.
Mama has stopped talking since Abuela died,
or else she would tell her to stay away
from Junior. She bleeds a little
then it stops and comes back.
She will not see a doctor.

Junior brings her flowers and then disappears,
some say back to Puerto Rico to find his daughter.
She can't remember Puerto Rico.
She winds the music box up,
sits and stares at the ballerina
whose left arm is missing.
She throws away her coat.

From the television she learns
the proper way to use a knife
and spends her evenings cutting carrots
into tiny tropical flowers
to put in her soup. Mama smiles.

Summer comes and she opens
all the windows and doors.
Junior comes back, alone, dark
and beautiful. She goes
to his house to listen to rumba.
The music box is silent again.
She bleeds a little then it stops.

You Will Learn Some Lessons Along the Way

The sky is a blackboard
where I once wrote
A girl is her own production
one hundred times.
The r, the teacher said, was too rolling.
She made me start over again
until it was rigid
like shrimp on a white dinner plate,
restrictive, redundant,
it felt like so many bridges
in a city gone to ruin,
like me leaning toward
my young love, unrequited.

With My Sacred Heart

From the window on the second floor
I saw the pine trees

and thought about the war,
Anne and the annex.

I can't remember if this class was before
or after mass,

when I was the star student
each week in God.

Hand over hand I received my rewards,
white squares of paper, each with a floating heart,

something like a locket that meant I belonged:
there was/is faith in faith,

in drawing circles on the laminate desks,
one inside the other,

mimicking a ripple, a knocking at the door,
the needle into the record's center—

Here, I daydreamed until my drawings trailed off
like a heart line, my connection broken,

and I was restored to the English teacher
who tirelessly scratched into the patina

on the wall, marking off
the days, white slashes like paper cuts,

and in between the rules
and the exceptions that proved them.

At Fifteen

Counting backward from ten, I'm lost
at one: it was meant to calm me down, like
an apology or shaking a snow globe,
but I have to start again, replaying the song
that speaks to my reverie. I drift
from my wish, the candles, a burning forest
now. The pearl in the box, a piece of that
burning. *Will I always be the sum
of my poverty?* Last night, I woke
to that, from the dream of hammering
a copper star in a whitewashed room.
I hadn't washed my hair for weeks. I guess
from the despair. It's amazing: after so little,
or so much, I think of the possibilities.

The Tethering Post

Still there from girlhood, aligning the sidewalks
like pins on a laundry rope, stand the tethering posts
in the shape of their intended possessions. Even then,

they had long since lost their use, left
as beacons of memory, stern in their neglect,
cauldron black, their iron mouths

biting down on the hoops that fell backward
like knockers on unused front doors.
What possessed me to kiss one?—

that metal taste like the brine of an olive
stayed with me long after I stopped twirling
around it as if it were my mother's leg.

Caning

One skill is given up for another: that summer
at the Cape it was caning that my grandfather,
who was more of a father, mastered.

I woke in the midnight hours to stutter
down the stairs in my eyelet nightgown
to the workroom where he was hunched

like a medic over an old chair frame.
I watched as he pulled and slid
slivers of wood inside each other

like so many sentences slipping
from his misplaced directions.
When he tightened the strands he leaned

back as if pulling on reins, the horse
the night before him when silence
magnifies the anticipation of sound,

interlude at the orchestra.
My grandfather's hands, the conductor's,
white as Carrara marble under the work light.

Each hole he made a honeycomb I could poke
my pinky through, but not by summer's end,
although I would not stop trying.

My grandfather rubbed his hands across
his own work when he was done, the screen
as against the confessor,

but he noticed it only as sky,
the grid and pattern of stars and night,
like fauna through the trees,

the lines and loops, an interlocking lace, brocade,
like so many ears in an auditorium rotunda,
crowding to hear such intimacies.

Latchkey I

You are lucky when you find fall in summer!
I remember finding it

in the right-hand corner
of the window at the head of my bed,
a crack in the shape of a dove
that let the wind through in a whistle—

a kind of origami. It seemed
to say, *You belong*
to no one but how you are
wanted,

if you want to be
wanted. But perhaps you can't control this,
any more than a wave
its resplendent blue belonging.

When You Find My Neighbor Elena, She'll Be Wearing the Classic Black Dress

and standing in front of a backdrop
of lattice, vines growing rampant in and out of the squares,
her own hair swimming. You'll know

she's just stopped running, even though she'll try her best to hide it:
you'll see how she's gasping for air, her mouth wide open
as if to say she's surprised to see you,
but she won't be at all, not really.
She's expected you to come, to have followed her from the boat
to the weathered house where she lives with her brother and his dog
and fries eggs in a well of bacon fat,
eating them straight from the skillet resting on a pillow in her lap,
the dog at her side like the plaster grizzly bear
frozen midleap on the left side of the sofa.
She'll sing to them, an octave too high but sweetly,
when she's drunk and crying.

She knows you watch her because she's so thin,
as thin as her mother, able to buy things in secondhand stores
and look good in them. Sometimes you catch her speaking
in Hungarian, like her mother, but she quickly smiles
that caught smile and looks away. When she buys bread
from the man who, like you, knows who she is, exactly,
she doesn't say thank you but just stares at him,
like she would an old lover.

You both live in the part of the city where the travelers come,
where the river turns, a muddy, dank river no one would swim in,
one only good enough for spit. Sometimes a group of men stand
together to see whose saliva will go the farthest.

When you approach her door with your gifts, you are thankful
to have a purpose, a destination at the end of the week,
and she, too, is grateful. She is dressed for you, dressed like a sliver
of the night you love her in, arms outstretched for the roses, the meats,
you saying, mimicking her accent, *You make the most tender steaks.*

Heidi's Hair Like Ivy

The ivy grows stronger in neglect,
scales the walls, becomes reptilian:

beauty does that, unleashes like
the disinherited. This is why she cut

off the wave of her hair in one stroke
and held it out like freshly caught prey.

But her father sent her to a summer
in her room, making her wear her hair in a bun

until it grew back as long as her spine
to divide her. In the fall she danced

the Ländler in full regalia with her brother,
her father pressing the accordion

in and out like lungs pressing oxygen.
Her hair whipped around her in the twist

of their arms, their push and pull,
our applause into prayers. At school,

we were the girls who loved her most,
who had combed her corn-silk hair:

who knew how we were
always trouble to ourselves.

Safe in the Kitchen

Today, the city
won't brighten

but remains a guillotine gray—
a day for alibis.

The river washed out.
There is nothing to be reflected,

just recovered,
like her body

from what they did.

The Compact

At sixty, my American grandmother had already given up
work and dress-up, but she still kept a compact in her purse,
put there with the sadness, a column of lipstick,

fuchsia like the azaleas she picked, rolling the petals
between her thumb and forefinger into tiny pellets
no bigger than the sleep in the corner of her eye.

They made her fingertips damp, as if she had
just licked them to turn a page in the book she read
to fall asleep. When she did, I opened the compact,

as if opening a letter, to find her fingerprints
and a bit of fuchsia in the center, where I studied
my mouth, a bridge, a torn leaf.

Writing Her Dissertation

The keys at night hammered out a word
like any key that unlocks
emptiness
from emptiness
in the pendulum of trying to belong—
no different than love,
or the threat of it.

Something almost said
was so easily lost to the incinerator,
burned like evidence,
no more than that.

My Mother's Dresden Teacup

On the hull there are tiny golden silhouettes
of a man and a woman standing inside a blue egg
and above it, a golden rim that carousels around

like a wedding band. It was perhaps a wedding
gift, en suite to a larger service with courtiers
and a king and queen prominently centered

on the tureen. Alone, now, they are all that is left:
he bowing just before or after a dance, holding
what appears to be her hand at first look

but is part of her skirt, as if he were
about to unthread her, pulling her out like a top
into a rotation, into a tiny planet, until she is

completely nude like the inside of the teacup,
porcelain white like a cameo. But the momentum
is caught like her elongated neck that swims

out toward him in that blue, what looks to be
a singular feather rising from her head, their toes
almost touching. Neither one is changed

when the hot tea is poured behind them, there is
no magic transformation like when my souvenir mug
turns a San Francisco blackened heart red.

The tea just darkens there with its prophecies,
clinging to the shell as my mother tilts
the cup to her mouth and watches *Doctor Zhivago*

on the small kitchen TV in the dark, reminding me
it was filmed mostly in Spain, as snow dissolves
into spring flowers, then Lara's face.

By the Trolley Line

My mother's house still stands
by the trolley line
where each passing trembles
a little life away: glass breaks
and falls to the kitchen floor.

I would wake on Sundays,
bathe in the shallow
claw-foot tub, feel the shift.
My mother came to tame
my hair, to lighten it.
In the kitchen, we spoke
of sleep, of mending
the old wooden stairs.

I do recall these things;
they don't recall me.
Even when I stand in the same
place, sit in the kitchen's fire,
it's my mother's hands I know,
not my face against them.

Souvenir

In the blues song the piano mimics
the train's passing over its tracks, the silverware

being polished for company, the crow spiraling downward
to get a closer look at what stirs in the bushes:

all of it a kind of muttering,
bodies burning in the dark against each other

in what becomes luck or misfortune,
and no matter what

happens, it happens. I am
such a souvenir, something brought up

from the wreckage, a negotiation that would not be
settled, a henceforth, a charm.

II. The Waiting Room

Having Witnessed the Illusion

A thin line of flesh outlined the geisha's mask, as if her face
were growing, but it was meant to entice,
to reveal just enough to say there was more

in the way a knitted sweater is a series of portholes,
and the body, the ocean, the thing contained
in its projection, a ship in a bottle, a cancer in its cell,

or the waiting room itself, where, from airport-like windows,
children are watched in a play yard
as they cross one another like an eclipse.

Through the Lens

I'm looking through it again,
seeing the distance emerge with neglect,
moving against this stillness
of its portrait
that is the self
in a country I have never been to,
where I look over rooftops,
where the world hardens in sunlight.
Suddenly, I'm the girl in the alcove
too poor for my questions,
collecting marbles instead:
one a periwinkle
with something inside,
caught in its falling,
like a glance between lovers at church,
something like a fossil,
indistinguishable from feather or bone.

The Hour

It's the flower pressed to fragility
to mark a page I won't share—

I'm smart enough to know
that the narrative is plenty

to bring me closer to myself,
smart enough not to want

a husband who will make me unfaithful.
I'm happy just to feel the flower

against my skin like a moth:
when my eyes are closed

I can't tell the difference,
both like paper torn from a worn book.

My Mother and I Tour the World While She Is Dying

Today, my mouth is full of glass,
broken Venetian flowers in the magazine,

like those things you almost say but don't.
Will these broken pieces

take shape, become the fragments
 of something more holy, stained

in the light? A bird here drowns in her red.
A bird here burns in her black.

My mouth here my empty pocket.

The Scrimshaw Begins to Glow in the Sun, on the Bedside Table

It is the slit of boredom or procrastination
                        that staggers into memory and chips away
at itself, the letter that cannot be sent
                        because of the sea, a rehearsal that becomes
the performance, the shadow that grows as light approaches
                        into a great cape rising like a sail behind you.

The Eye Exam

I understand how knives are fish,
what the student said to me yesterday,
as if he knew that today I would be part wolf

when they dropped tears into my eyes
and left me to change,
almost forgetting what they had done.

Then I became the peephole,
the shape of things almost visible
in the distance, when they become

what you need them to be, maybe
even the thing that disassembles
in order to suit itself—

like knife to fish to knife. Afterward,
everything was brighter
like an x-ray pushed against light bulbs,

my old face in the vanity. The anomalies
like someone walking right behind you.
Someone whose features

you will never recall, who stands there
just slightly out of sight, who turns out the lights
so that you may see more clearly.

Her Life on the Wall

The curtain frames the window

like the hair did her face

in the portrait of that unnamed girl

on the wall those many years.

Behind her, cracks ran up and down—

trees in the river, ripening the water.

Notes from the Forest

The desperation of Friday night, the lingering
canopy of our trouble

gives us this soft moment, a watery content
inside where I turn again to look

in the pocket mirror, just the left eye
because that is like looking back—

back into a canvas where a fingernail
carved a moon's spine bent over like a hunch,

which is the projection of my own that I can't
articulate, not yet, not as I'll come to know it—

salivating with what is sour and sweet and dark—
searching, like my mother, for another detective show.

MRI

My mother is the even line that is
the pen dashing across a rectangle of ice.

Closing her eyes, she says, *It's night, Alpha
Centauri, perpetual night.* She thinks

the heart must darken as it ages, like a chestnut
as it is baked. *That smell,* she thinks,

is like the old. She wants to ask them if the heart
grows darker with time, but she won't, fearing

what they will think of her. She wants to see
my children grow. She wants . . . She must

be alone for them to see what is inside her,
in the way you must be further to see more,

above, to see below. As she goes, she says when
I was a girl I told her that sometimes

the world shines looking back at you like a plate
staring up from the table, with you in its glaze.

The Streak

The white iris
pressed in your book,

yellowed by distance,
like a voice from the memory

that is summer,
that LP, that LP.
I'm running with that heartbeat.
Don't tell me it is too late:
I know it is.

When You Were Mine.

The book smells of tobacco.
Nights smelled of tobacco.

Your nurse smells of it.
Coming in from the rain,

it's as strong as love
and how we remember it.

Child on a Tricycle

My first baby grew no larger than a grain of rice
puffed from the heat,
curled like a pinky on a writer's hand.

They said it was gone before it left
my body and sent it home with me like a grade.

We went to a diner in an old trolley car.
I had tea and toast:
the provisions of sickness.
The city streets stretched out before us
like so many long equations.

I thought of my womb as a cul-de-sac
where a child would ride her tricycle
in that rotation of nearing home to pass it.

Latchkey 2

I came upon the house,
randomly, as if to a page,
perfect like it was

without knowing,
like inside the snow globe
that meant how I was

where I needed to be,
a stillness in a museum,
eyes darting back and forth

and through the canvas
in that literacy of being inside,
of just being in it so deeply

I became that answer
boomeranging back at myself
and out as in light—yes,

the clarity, like light from that
simple house, flickering
at the train's passengers.

After the Miscarriage,
I Drove to the Playground

They pull up in a red pickup, the girl straddled across her father's lap,
her head tucked beneath his chin, a pink pacifier plugging up
her four-year-old mouth, as if she were a sink full of water.

They fall out of the truck and into the November air, and she skips
ahead to the playground. *Slow down*, he says, *Kelly girl*.
She throws her head back, in the way her mother must.

Her arms are shiny in the sunlight, as if someone had rubbed oil
on them. But the rest of her is covered with a powdery dirt,
a thin dusting of cocoa. *Kelly girl want swing*, he says

as he lights a cigarette and pushes wildly until she is taut
with laughter. The pacifier falls out of her mouth to where
it is lost, and her dress flies upward to cover her face. *Enough*, he says.

When she gets down she is slower, as if just waking from a nap. The sun
bleeds orange across the sky, like fire seen through an oven's window.
You can almost taste it, in the winter, the sugar the body craves.

When My Mother Is Weeks Away from Leaving, Her Client Calls Her for Counsel

She wanted to tear the cloud to pieces,
wanted to pluck it out of the sky
and pull at it like she would a tissue or a carnation
in the pews or the dance halls,
anywhere she was
forced to see or hear things
in an arc of beginning, middle, and end
(why she came late or left early)
like a life or a song.

She wanted to hold a bird
like a feather
or a feather like a bird,
to hear one line of the song over and over
until she changed the words: *You are
my sunshine, my star, my light,
my luminous point, my drifting.*
She wanted to hand out pieces
of the cloud to all the men she knew
like greeting cards she sprayed
with light perfume,
soft as the tissue, as carnations
she shredded in lonely places
(which shifted by the minute).

She reread the poem out loud: *The cloud
is the past billowing past.* Once there was
a cord on the telephone
that she wrapped around her finger
like a ringlet of hair
she was so envious of—
that her daughter works so hard to straighten—
until she felt her pulse
as anxious as her cloudlike pet rabbit Alice
whom she loved to pieces.

Dying in Winter

The blue garden orb resists the snow.
Instead, it follows as an eye down the street,

as in the anticipation of a coronation,
or birth itself with the bearing down

and a mouthful of salt. It insists
and insists and organizes the world

around it. It hushes and opiates uniformly
like a church bell. It says that nothing

can be said differently, though we never
believe it. It says we are all stories. It goes

forgotten like a holiday gift. Children
stop to heat their hands above it, in that fire,

gaze into the future as if it were a possibility.
One girl bows her head to kiss it, of all things.

Moments in the Trees

My mother's owl face is becoming more owl-like,
something startled in the wilderness

when it hears a human voice,
even its own, like an unexpected

reflection in a windowpane
when the mind is years ago

in the village that no longer is
a village, thinking of that boy who no longer is

a boy. Her brow furls like someone
blowing into a reed

to push music through, tightening
the pitch into its eye, sharpening

until the voice is gone.
Then she looks at me with caution,

before her eyes close
again, for now.

Learning Silence

All day she's suckling,
a feral thing

that would eat itself
to death. She has become

what she once fed
under the wind chimes,

something that cannot
look at me, or is it I who cannot look

at her? The world in this light
is the truth of it, why

some girls cut themselves.
Close enough, her breath is the inside

of the cocoon we opened,
old books where flowers

are pushed in like tattoos
highlighting the longing.

Over the Waves

Cars pass and light up the wall,
casting spotlights that intertwine,

illuminating dancers in a music box
who turn away from each other

to find themselves, as if before a duel.
In this apparition, it's necessary for one

to leave in order for the other to remain,
or both would be lost: there

are certain truths, even when no one
wants to listen. So you must listen

more intently, in the way you looked
at the sky at fifteen, looking for what

belonged to you. Listen
to the circus music that burns from braille

where a finger is a little hammer
branding your surrender

to "Sobre las Olas," to the waltz
by which so many have moved

through the air, bullets of exaltation,
to that which cannot happen but is here.

My Mother Will Never Leave the Room Alive Again

The city blocks grow longer in walking,
as do the skyscrapers, like a man once
while sleeping as I watched, like dough
under the kitchen cloth. I take a breath in

for as long as I can, hold it like a lie.
I have built my tolerance. There is so much
the camera wants to see in its wash,
and nothing can end before it is meant.

The golden hour comes in, with its honey
and shafts. The ladders are taken down
or abandoned for the walk. The same birds
have moved overhead all day, unnoticed,

until now, like the brass bracelets sliding
on a woman's arm at the open bar,
and the beaded crimson earrings
that almost touch her shoulders or do

as she tilts her head to show she is listening,
tassels shaped like her own body, or ones
on an Arabian horse, or ones pulling back
curtains for a private view of the trees.

III. Reclaimed

Ticonderoga

An elusive thought wakes me to my eyes sealed with dust, turning them
lizard-like. Then I'm up for hours, peering over the same page
in a book that the tiny book lamp illuminates down like a miner's light.
This insomnia yields tomorrow's doldrums and a day lost to what is never
remembered. These are the days my mother said to *Just call out*. The ones
you sacrifice for the rest. I stop on the question that woke me, that dream,
its straining ambiguity that boiled up like fat. How did that dream
change me? How did it make me soft?

Earlier that night, my husband had touched my hand mistakenly,
startling me. I was thinking of the children walking the desert alone,
leaving the highlands in search of a new life, like the boy I tutored
English. Trucks first, then train hopping, and finally just on foot
to attempt to cross the border. He was thankful he hadn't had to sell
his body. *Sometimes people would touch you, just to show that they could, to say
you are nothing.* Yes, a touch could say that.

I was teaching him about primary sources and the American Revolution,
repeating for him the place Ticonderoga. I showed him
the school pencils with the same name, yellow and long. He said,
Like school buses. Narrow like arrows.

A day later, finally catching up to myself, I rose from my bed to care for
my growing children. They are hungry for this, for me, for the dough
I boil before I bake it into little golden nuggets. Some skip this step
when making little pretzels, but this is how I was taught. This is what
I was told makes them dark and chewy. The nuggets rise quickly,
like laughter. Then I bake them, and in moments they are devoured.
The children ask for more. I oblige, moving about it steadily, rhythmically.
It's my apology. My wish to be well. No longer can I take them in my bed
when I am lost. No longer can I watch them sleep together, counting
the number of their synchronized breaths like counts between thunder.
I miss the little one the most. How she would hold on to my hair, pulling
at it like a vine, as if she were swinging right through me.

My Son Learns Art Can Save Him

They sat next to each other
in kindergarten,
each day for an hour,
warming lines on paper
with what they almost knew,
and one day she drew God
following her to town,
so he drew himself
following God following her
to town, and bakeries and post offices
appeared, along with libraries
and fruit stands, coffee shops,
museums, and animals, all sorts,
even ones that didn't exist but did in this
binary born out of their belief
that God was there
between them,
like the air before a match is struck
and light is just torn from it,
ripped right into being,
into more days like the ones before,
when villages turned to cities
and cities back to fields,
always with one child looking ahead
and the other looking back
to find each other in the center.

The Quarry Inside Me

Each day now is a Sunday, the other side of what happened,
that huskiness of goodbye—

even when I say I am happy, I am
not, but pushing myself to believe, and it has to be enough,

like the way I hear my mother, from the well, the quarry
that is all an immigrant has of her dream,

the hole of it which becomes a life
in that symmetry of a thing and its absence.

Driving By

A slender hour to have alone,
to slip from the envelope
like the good advice she would offer:
There is only so much you can do.
I want to tell her that I know, know
how allegiance is its own deception.
It is better to speak in allegories.
For these brief months
the tree that I pass each night
is an arrow of stars
pointed straight toward the stars.
We can only feel so much.

Awakening to My Mother's Voice from Beyond

I'm not going to lie, I didn't like many men:
there was always something they wanted,
even more than love,
which was all I had to give.

Today I'm just listening to Peter, Paul and Mary's
"Early Morning Rain" over and over.
Now you can even watch them
whenever you want
in black and white,
those antiquated snapshots come to life,
as if you were a time traveler.

Maybe, hija, you should go to the
planetarium today and watch the universe
expanding, or marvel at Titan,
Saturn's largest moon with wind and rain,
and follow the constellations.
Outside, pay a cartoonist to draw you
as a caricature of yourself,
of all the ways you're imperfect,
and place it in a box to find years from now.

The Flora Print Still Hangs Above Her Bed

The truth becomes its lie
like how we are loved

in an impression of an impression,
a coin burned into dirt

or the pattern of an interpretation
that synchronizes itself

from desire—we can see it
in the trees, those tender palms

open for the offering or biding
their departure in the wind.

Mi Casa

I painted my house cerulean blue
like the house in my mother's story,

the one in her village, made of water,
where each night, the proprietor, a woman

doctor, so strange for the time and place,
plucked a fish right out of the walls, gutted it,

and fried it with capers, onions, and tomatoes.
It was a kind of willfulness: to feed oneself,

to be a woman doctor, to keep an ocean upright
like metal in flight. In this house, my mother said,

there were no masculine or feminine words,
the spoons were always joyous

and women always safe. The house didn't know
it was water any more than a child does.

Because it was always there, my mother said,
no one ever questioned why it was.

Votives

Soon it will be your birthday
and I will light

candles in a shaved-chocolate forest
and we will gather around

those little torches
that will bring us back

from the death voices,
one for each year, and the other

not for good luck
but for the year

that would have become
that luck.

Final Receipt

I have my mother's last
grocery bill in my wallet—
her canned peaches,
evaporated milk,
a measuring spoon,
as if she were
thinking about allusion,
how we must all return
to the sea, knowing
that all we are is
memory as she
wandered the aisle
in search of what caught her
beyond hesitation
that last time.

My Daughter Is Spending the Rest of the Summer in Her Room

Today, there is no one
but her
and the house gnome
she has conjured
to make her safe
and the little brooms
made of sticks, chicken bones,
and locks of her own
flaxen hair
that she strokes
against her face
in the way she once did mine
as she talks to her, our dead,
and sings,
waving a flashlight
around her room,
the dark room,
but for the circle of light
and its capacity.

Reclaimed

The month has begun
with its series of little doors,

each one opening to an illustration
of various forms of light.

Midway through the month, a boy
puckers his lips against a trumpet,

its rim illuminated into a halo,
or a ring polished into surprise,

an ideogram for looking
out a window,

finding hope in what it is
you hope for.

Because We Are Planets Swarming with Life

Even when my daughter sleeps she sings,
her eyes rushing back and forth
beneath the paperlike veil of flesh.

Sometimes she opens them
with a question,
but they are still locked into

the story of their release
and recoil like a mussel
from a finger. Just enough light

lingers from the windows,
to lift her from the dark canvas,
enough for me to see the scrawling

in my book—a dedication to some lost sister:
Once, the sister wrote, *we were the angels
in a Boar's Head Pageant, lifting silk*

*from arms into wings. It was there
I had the epiphany that there are creatures
inside us who dwell in our warmth.*

Faith and Practice

In the last bench in Meeting I am
all the other women and all of their silence

weaving and knitting and putting
clothes out to dry. Sometimes

I'm on the subway all those years ago
pressed against my mother

in growing, in those few moments of sleep
when waking restores the journey,

not the metaphorical one but the physical,
the tremor and sound like fireworks shooting

and air filling tires. Then the parting of doors,
the screech of it, which was anticipation

and forgetfulness, the fear and surety
of each other. The soot always in our eyes.

Then our long walk home to clean them.
Our restored conversation in midair.

Carnival

Tonight, the repetition is the change
by which I am measured.

I tell my children I am too old,
no, too worn

out, like the carnies.
No, they are beautiful:

I was wrong. I was insolent.
Everything is almost,

and that's the glint,
like you my brave ones

in the light, eager
to win something.

The Rhyme Game

Shimmy shimmy ko-ko bop
Shimmy shimmy bop
Near the last day of camp
twelve-year-old girls chant from the picnic bench,
others joining in the circle when their mothers
in high heels drop them off,
barely stopping before
the princess wave goodbye.

Shimmy shimmy ko-ko bop
The girls are learning to say fuck-me heels
through giggles,
arching their feet and eyebrows.
Shimmy shimmy ko-ko bop
Lips purse into a push of air on the *p*.
They slap themselves and each other silly
in the rhyme game, words altered.
Shimmy shimmy cocoa pop
Shimmy shimmy cocoa pop
They bump each other,
play chicken in the pool, spit.
Down down baby
Down down baby
One girl fake-drowns
into a lifeguard's scream
and they are all banned for an hour.

In the locker room they stand
in front of a mirror like the Rockettes
in a kickline, the tallest in the middle
and the smallest at the end,
into Hadrian's arch.
They suck in their bellies, grow
disproportionate
as in a funhouse mirror.
Skinny skinny cocoa puff
Skinny skinny cocoa puff
Breast pop like Skipper's
with a twist of her arm
as if winding a clock.

Their arms cross over chests
to make an X of the dying.
Sweet, sweet baby, I'll never let you go

They shimmy back out into the sun,
squinting at the flash of light
until their eyes readjust
and they find each other again
to make another circle,
shaking their hips.
Ding-dong hot dog
A man turns to his wife,
asking if she could tell any of them apart.
She winces and shakes *Nos* back to her book.

Put it all backwards and what do you get?
They sing, clap, and line up again
to collapse like dominoes with the last
days of trust pushing up against each other.

Canción

The Black Angus converge
under the Joshua tree,
raven black, darker
than their own shadows,
a pool of themselves
that is the well, the word,
the cool echo that enters as *thee*
and comes back up as *thou*.

The Descendants

Someday they will reinvent us
around an evening table,
see us as pioneers,
better than them,
or the best they have to offer.
They will pick up porcelain
and stroke it like St. Peter's foot
as they find our names
in a letter, on a photograph,
and pause looking at it like a painting.
One will say
that we are inside of them
like the burning drink
that makes them well
with that blush between sorrow
and happiness
that comes in the second
of one year moving into another,
that draws
the closest body to yours.

When We Were Immortal

—after The Starry Night

The wind is curled there or is it breath
like that of you in my ear when we were
then in that consumption of us? Each
fascination drew us back
to the heaviness of it, the smoke of it
in winter billowing out of our kindling.
It was the tapping to the sessions,
the goblets clanging, fingerprints
on the cutlery. It was the instrument of being
the one, the perfection that only hands
can realize. To be pressed to a wall
was to open into a window
in a room with only one door, which
was locked. Each inaccurate perception
a sustaining truth, for all our lifetime.
A whole village asleep inside us
with the mistral wind and its cleansing.

Fridays, I Stop to Read Their Journals

My student wrote in her marble notebook
in parentheses, *I am
just a paraphrase of you!*
The exclamation like helium
lifting the *you* up inside,
pulling it like a leash. Small
doodles dance around the words
like debris in a tornado: hearts,
flowers, an eye with thick
darkened lashes that say
two eyes are never enough.
There are no grades for this
discernment, but my returning
doodle of a full sun
with finlike rays overlapping
each other and a smiley face
inside that she will later
mistake for a starfish.

Candlemas

Today, the sky was a white flag of surrender,
torn at the edges, a ruffled bandage,
wedding dress pulled from a cedar chest,
smelling of salt and pekoe tea. It's always
the end of the journey that is the longest.

I drove behind an old meat purveyor truck,
boxy like an ambulance but wintergreen,
with wind chimes hanging in the back,
striking at a stop with the frenzy
of a doorbell at an unanswered door.

A strange cartoonish cow's face beamed
from the fender as old as the meat truck,
before my childhood, suggesting
I'm happiest when smiling. The chimes
kept hitting glass at each false start.

Was there any meat in there at all?
On the streets, the Christmas
ornaments were almost all taken down,
except for a few lone houses
that held on like mothers, and one still

with a lit tree standing in the bay window.
Would I ever go outside if I didn't have to?
The lights quivered on and off and on.
As the truck turned into its lost direction,
words ran fresh from a long time.

Sorting Through My Inheritance

Sometimes there's no translation.
A word so much a word that you can't speak it. More taste. Filament.
When everyone else is sleeping I think of you
writing postcards, trying to maximize space, get as close to your meaning:
Pine trees smell like I thought they would, like a cure.
Together, the most beautiful words in the English language are 'cellar door.'
It's called, *Euphony.*
You heard it somewhere.
You were always listening with your elfin ears.
I told you that cellar door didn't sound English and that's why you liked it.
You told me there's so much deception you must make your own truth.
You said I was as beautiful as the words, or any.
I thought I was a cellar.
All through adolescence, I was always both awake and asleep.
You would ask me: *¿Entiendes?*
Then quickly remembered English: *Do you understand?*
Entiendo, Mamá.
¿Entiendes?
After you are dead, I'm happiest becoming you.

Epilogue

I painted these wooden boxes deep burgundy—
as if I were the child again, not her mother.

I painted them like my own lips and cheeks
in dress-up, painted them

like the trees in the woods in spring,
our springs in the North. Here, I put the stories

back, returned wood to wood, drew
the shutters in against the sun like a slap

that sends the birds flying. The smallest
muñeca was there with me, the last one

to hear the stories, who said, *Let's put
them in the cuckoo clock.* So we sealed

them in the attic. Then we went to the fields
to be with the horses, but we could only hear them.

The smallest muñeca said to me,
You can't tell if they're coming or going.

No, my lovely little nut, I said,
they are one and the same.

Notes

I.

"Mine": The Spanish words translated to English are *tía* to *aunt*, *azul* to *blue*, *hija* to *daughter*, and *mía* to *mine*.

"You Will Learn Some Lessons Along the Way" is in my mother's voice.

"Writing Her Dissertation" is dedicated to all the women, including my mother, who did not finish their PhD dissertations because they lacked support.

"My Mother's Dresden Teacup": The lines "there is / no magic transformation like when my souvenir mug / turns a San Francisco blackened heart red" refers to mugs popular in the 1980s that changed form when hot water was poured into them. The movie *Doctor Zhivago* is based on the Russian book by Boris Pasternak of the same title and named for the protagonist, a doctor and a poet. The movie takes place in Moscow and Siberia but was filmed, in large part, in Spain.

"By the Trolley Line" refers to Norristown High Speed Line, formerly known as the Philadelphia and Western Railway, the P&W, also known as Route 100. From the 1930s to the 1990s, the cars, high-speed trolleys, were aluminum bullet cars. Originally steam cars, they were converted to third-rail electric cars. They averaged eighty miles an hour, with open windows through spring and summer, and the ride produced sound and vibration much like being on a wooden roller coaster. It passed just yards from my house, and I rode it regularly.

II.

"MRI": Alpha Centauri is a triple-star system four light-years away. The stars in Alpha Centauri include two stars, AB, that orbit close to each other. They are both similar to our own sun, though B is smaller and not as bright. The image of these stars is central to the Alpha Centauri reference in this poem.

"The Streak": The line *"When You Were Mine"* refers to the song by Prince but made popular by Cyndi Lauper on her debut album, *She's So Unusual*, 1983, Portrait Records, and how hearing a song returns us to not only a physical location but who we were then.

"Over the Waves" translates to "Sobre las Olas," the famous waltz by Mexican composer Juventino Rosas and synonymous with circuses, fairgrounds, and visions of the Wild West.

III.

"Awakening to My Mother's Voice from Beyond" is in my mother's voice and celebrates her love of YouTube.

"Because We Are Planets Swarming with Life" came after I watched the Boar's Head Pageant my husband pipes in each year, at St. Peter's Lutheran Church in Lafayette Hill, Pennsylvania. Boar's Head Festivals are thought to date back to pagan times but were linked to Christianity in Medieval England. Prominent noblemen and families served the pork for Christmas and engaged in heavy drinking. The pork required a lot of preparation and serving it often involved a procession that included minstrels, huntsmen, and servants. The Puritans put an end to these indulgences, and the festival never returned as a custom. Some churches and organizations hold yearly festivals with a synthetic boar's head, along with Christmas music and the presentation of the Christ child.

"Faith and Practice" shares its name with the Yearly Meeting of the Religious Society of Friends book, which serves as "guide" for members on the practice of being a Quaker. The work of practice is something my mother was highly attuned to, and she guided me to the understanding that almost everything is about how we carry out our beliefs in the world. Faith, in whatever form, is repleted by such execution.

"The Rhyme Game": *"Shimmy Shimmy, Ko-Ko-Bop"* is the title of a song recorded by Little Anthony and the Imperials in 1959, adapted by Bob Smith from a song written and recorded by El Capris in 1956. It went on to be covered by several bands, including Urban Guerillas in 1983, when I was thirteen. The song objectifies a "native girl" and exemplifies how young girls are exposed to a misogynistic culture that gets into their psyches. Skipper refers to Barbie's younger sister, introduced by Mattel in 1964. Growing Up Skipper was released in the 1970s. When her arm was rotated, her breasts popped out, and she grew and slenderized so she could, as the commercial promised, "wear her glamorous teenage skirt."

"Canción" translates to *song* in Spanish.

"When We Were Immortal": Mistral wind refers to the cold, dry northwest wind that blows through the Rhone Valley to the Mediterranean, predominantly in the winter and spring, heightening between seasons. It usually lasts only one or a few days and brings clear weather in its wake. It is the wind I think of when I see *The Starry Night*.

"Epilogue": The Spanish word *muñeca* translates to *doll*.

About the Author

Nicole Greaves holds an MFA from Columbia University and an MEd from Chestnut Hill College. Her poetry has appeared in numerous literary reviews and was awarded prizes by the Academy of American Poets and the Leeway Foundation of Philadelphia. She was a 2015 finalist for the Coniston Prize of *Radar Poetry,* who also nominated her for Best of the Net. In 2020, she was a finalist for the Frontier Digital Chapbook Contest and the Dogfish Head Poetry Contest. Nicole is Poet Laureate Emeritus of Montgomery County, Pennsylvania, and she currently teaches English and creative writing in Philadelphia. Nicole's mother came to the US from Panama at seventeen, and they lived a life on the margins. Much of her work explores themes relating to this experience, specifically the tensions around acculturation, gender roles, and class. *Having Witnessed the Illusion* is her first book.

Glass Lyre Press

exceptional works to replenish the spirit

Glass Lyre Press is an independent literary publisher interested in technically accomplished, stylistically distinct, and original work. Glass Lyre seeks diverse writers that possess a dynamic aesthetic and an ability to emotionally and intellectually engage a wide audience of readers.

Glass Lyre's vision is to connect the world through language and art. We hope to expand the scope of poetry and short fiction for the general reader through exceptionally well-written books, which evoke emotion, provide insight, and resonate with the human spirit.

Poetry Collections
Poetry Chapbooks
Select Short & Flash Fiction
Anthologies

www.GlassLyrePress.com

www.ingramcontent.com/pod-product-compliance
Lightning Source LLC
Chambersburg PA
CBHW022013120526
44592CB00034B/803